This book belongs to:

....

Mrs Wordsmith®

RECEPTION ENGLISH

COLOSSAL WORKBOOK

Bearnice

Bogart

Brick

Plato

Grit

Yin & Yang

Armie

Shang High

Oz

MEET THE
CHARACTERS

CONTENTS

LETTERS & SOUNDS

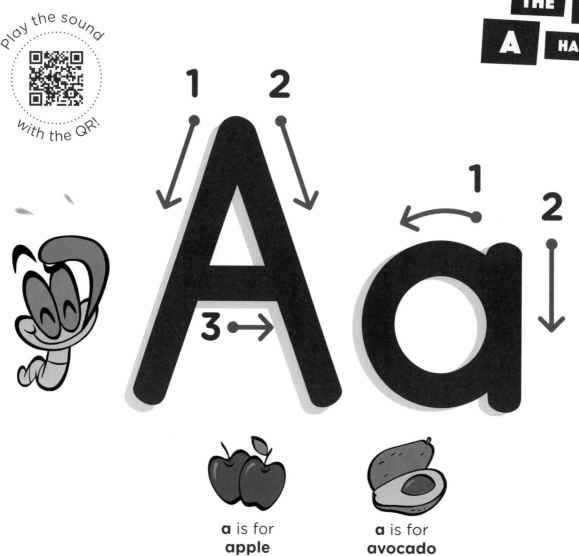

a is for
apple

a is for
avocado

TRY IT

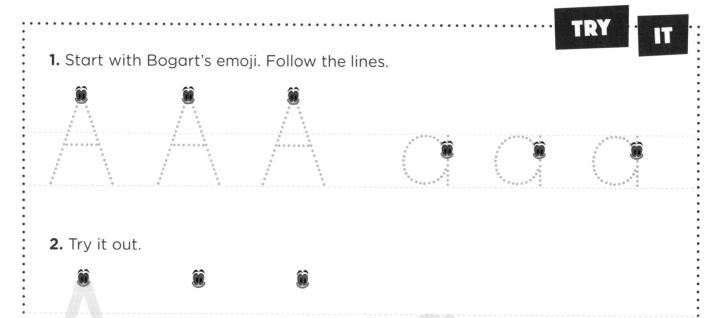

1. Start with Bogart's emoji. Follow the lines.

2. Try it out.

Play the sound with the QR!

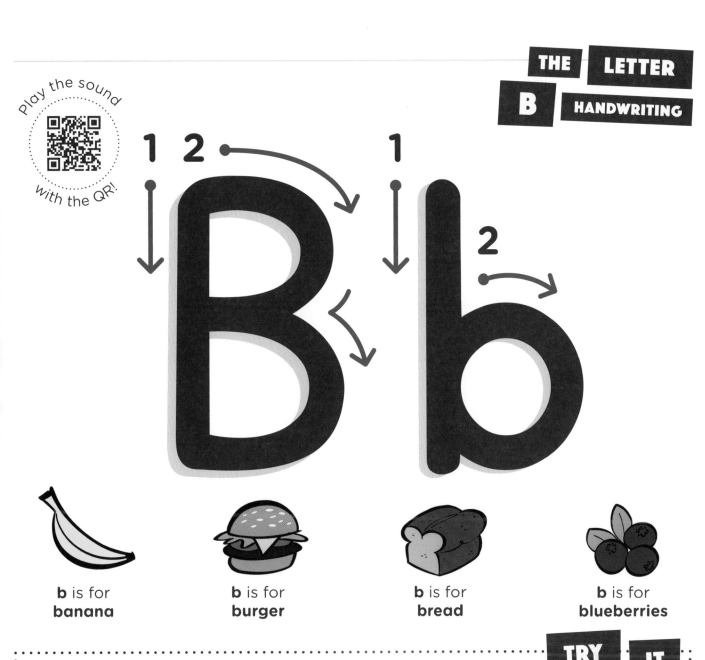

b is for
banana

b is for
burger

b is for
bread

b is for
blueberries

TRY IT

1. Start with Bogart's emoji. Follow the lines.

2. Try it out.

Play the sound with the QR!

c is for
cake

c is for
carrot

c is for
cabbage

c is for
corn

TRY IT

1. Start with Bogart's emoji. Follow the lines.

2. Try it out.

Play the sound with the QR!

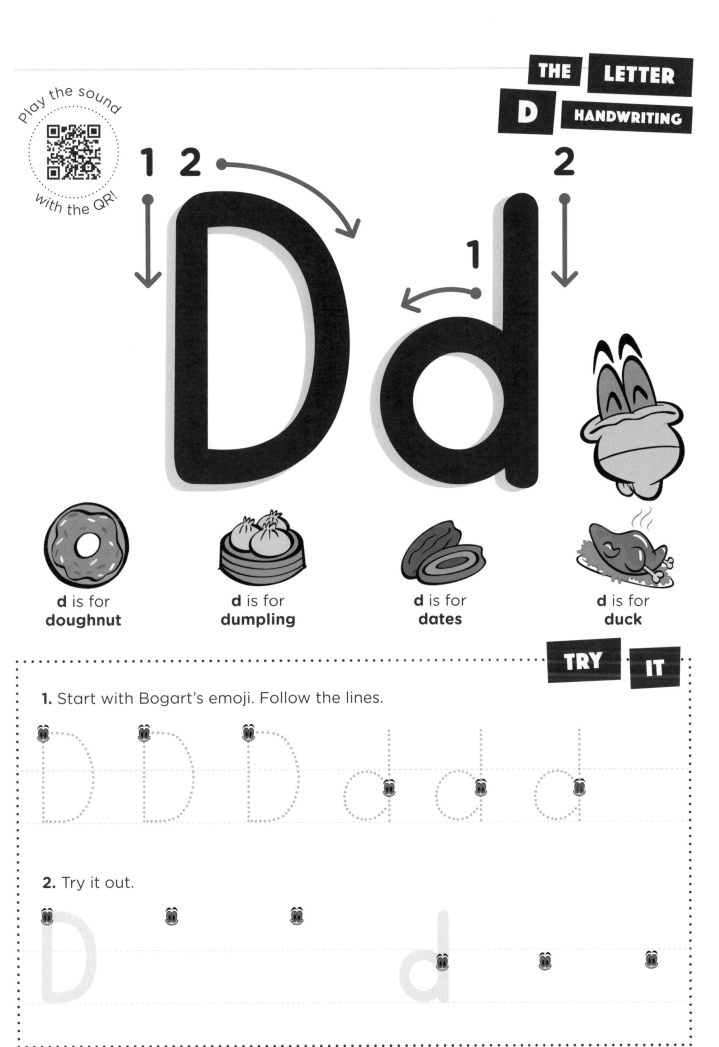

1 2 **2** **1**

d is for
doughnut

d is for
dumpling

d is for
dates

d is for
duck

1. Start with Bogart's emoji. Follow the lines.

D D D d d d

2. Try it out.

D   d

Play the sound with the QR!

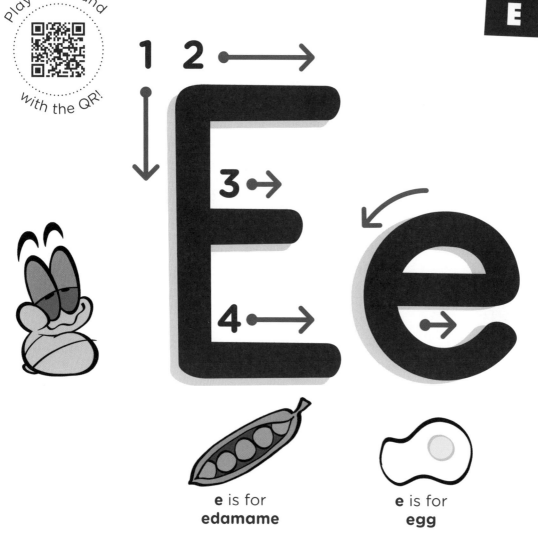

e is for
edamame

e is for
egg

1. Start with Bogart's emoji. Follow the lines.

2. Try it out.

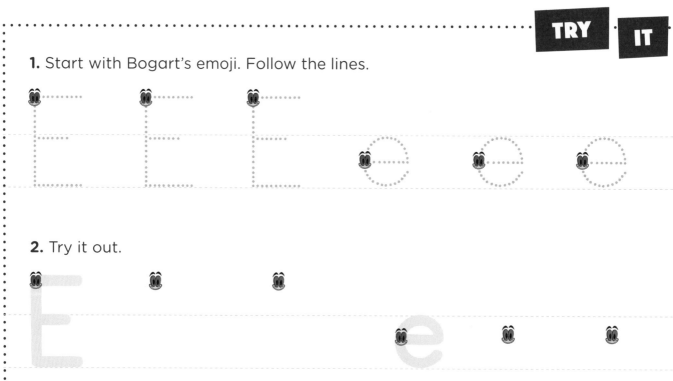

Play the sound
with the QR!

1 **2** ⟶

F **3**→

2→ **f** **1**

f is for
falafel

f is for
figs

f is for
flour

f is for
fries

TRY IT

1. Start with Bogart's emoji. Follow the lines.

2. Try it out.

Play the sound with the QR!

g is for
granola

g is for
grapefruit

g is for
grapes

g is for
garlic

TRY IT

1. Start with Bogart's emoji. Follow the lines.

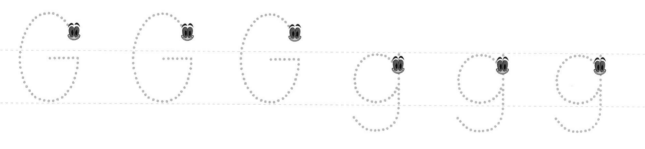

2. Try it out.

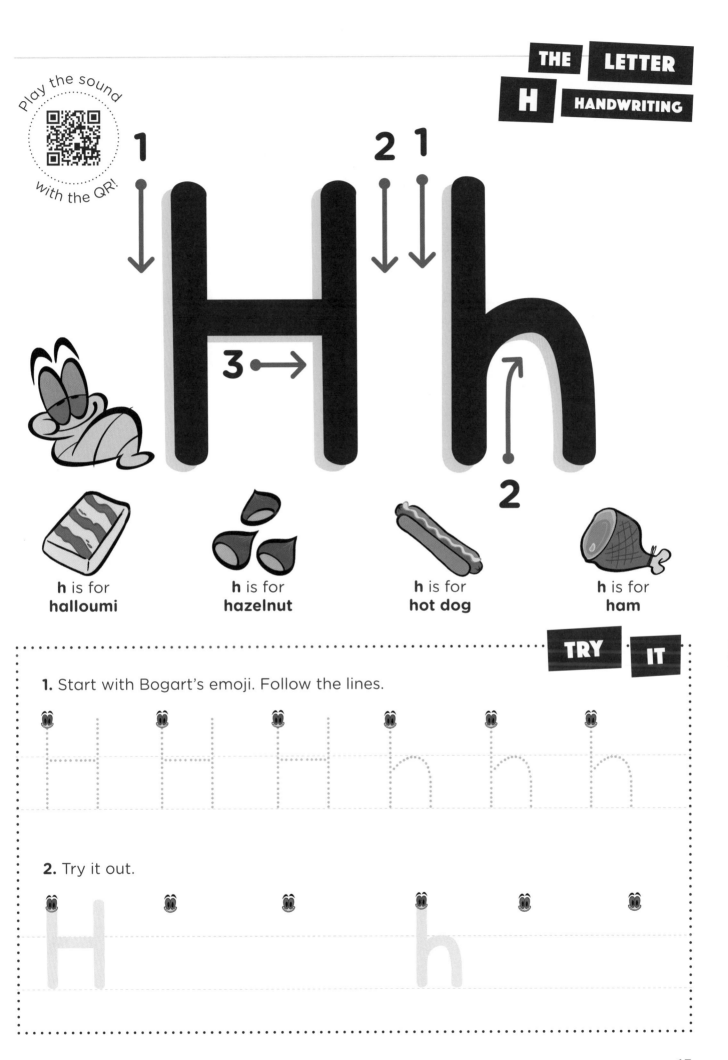

Play the sound with the QR!

1

2 1

3 →

2

h is for
halloumi

h is for
hazelnut

h is for
hot dog

h is for
ham

TRY IT

1. Start with Bogart's emoji. Follow the lines.

2. Try it out.

15

Play the sound with the QR!

2 →

1 ↓

DOT

Ii

3 →

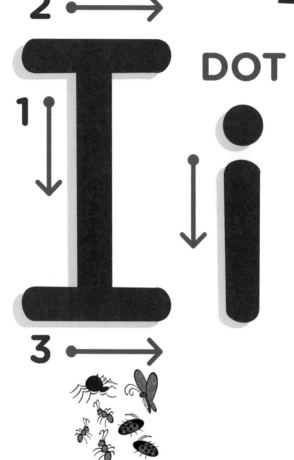

i is for
insects

1. Start with Bogart's emoji. Follow the lines.

2. Try it out.

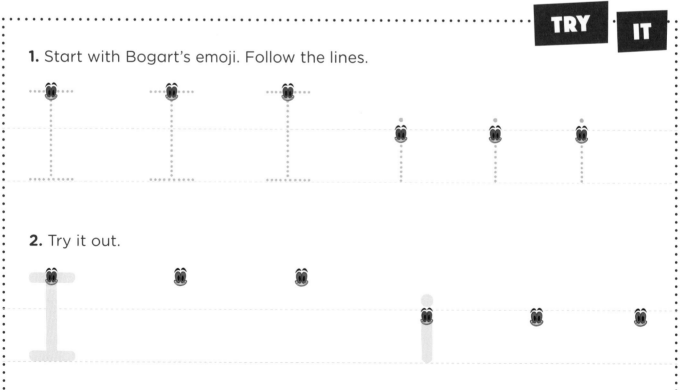

16

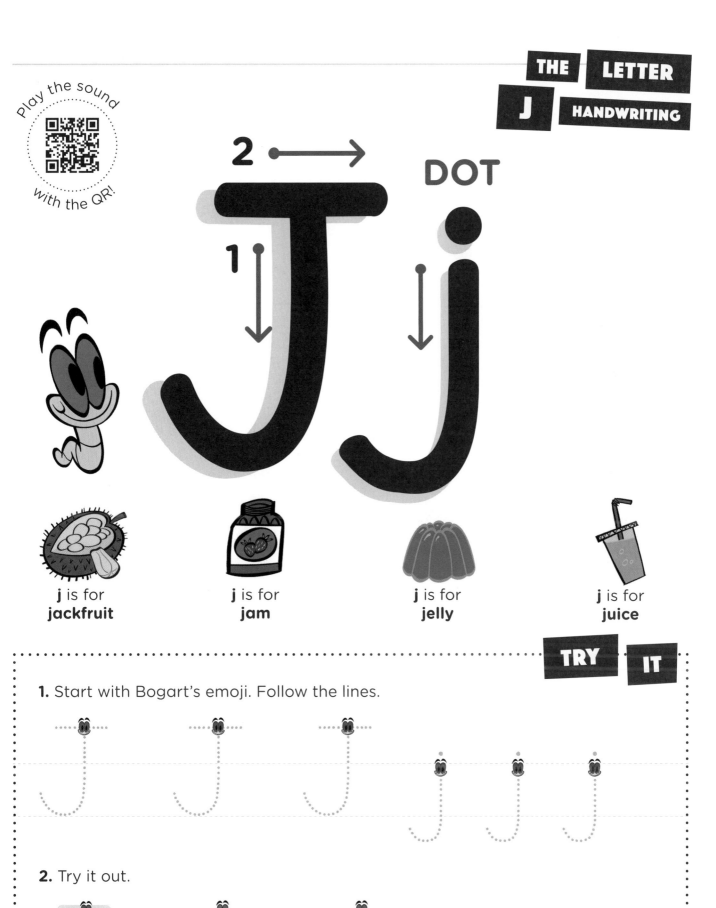

2 →

1

DOT

j is for **jackfruit**

j is for **jam**

j is for **jelly**

j is for **juice**

TRY IT

1. Start with Bogart's emoji. Follow the lines.

2. Try it out.

Play the sound with the QR!

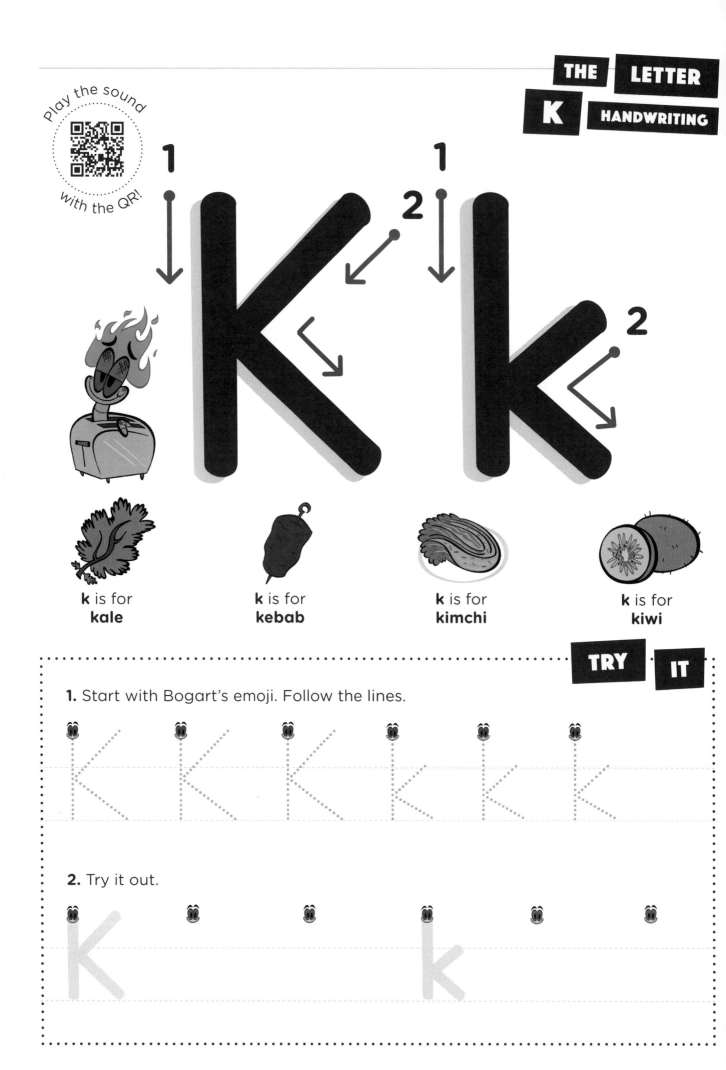

k is for **kale**

k is for **kebab**

k is for **kimchi**

k is for **kiwi**

TRY IT

1. Start with Bogart's emoji. Follow the lines.

2. Try it out.

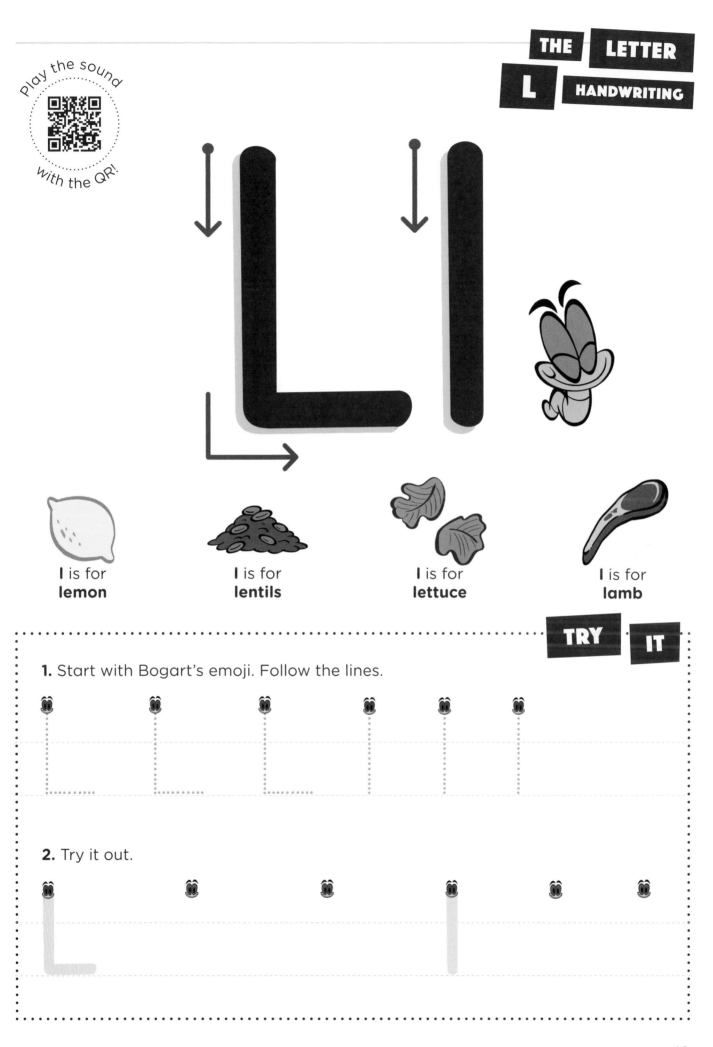

Play the sound with the QR!

l is for **lemon**

l is for **lentils**

l is for **lettuce**

l is for **lamb**

TRY IT

1. Start with Bogart's emoji. Follow the lines.

2. Try it out.

Play the sound with the QR!

1 2 1

m 2 3

m is for **macaron**

m is for **meatballs**

m is for **mushroom**

m is for **mustard**

TRY IT

1. Start with Bogart's emoji. Follow the lines.

2. Try it out.

Play the sound with the QR!

n is for
nettles

n is for
nuts

1. Start with Bogart's emoji. Follow the lines.

2. Try it out.

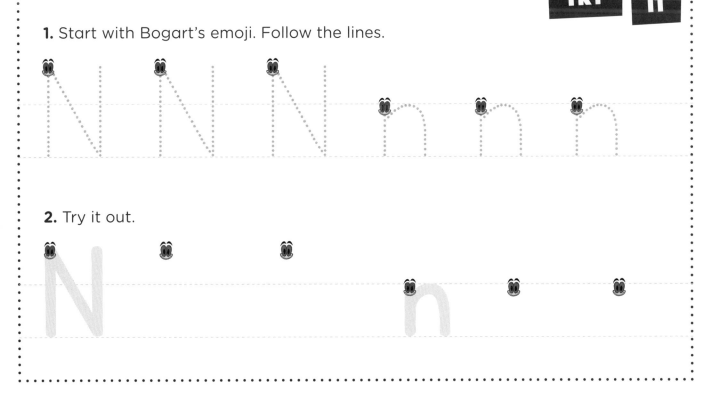

o is for
orange juice

o is for
olive oil

o is for
olives

TRY IT

1. Start with Bogart's emoji. Follow the lines.

2. Try it out.

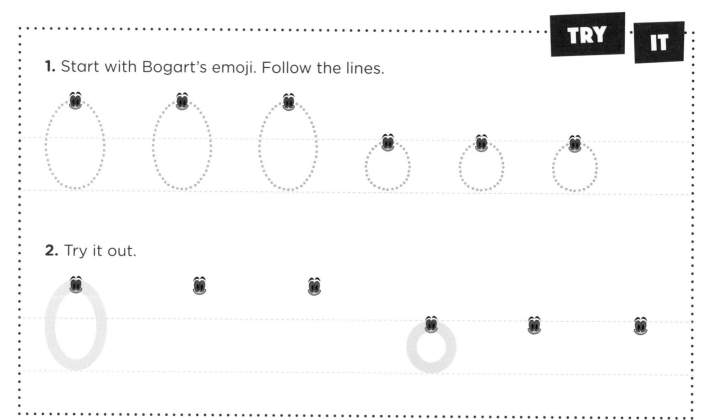

Play the sound with the QR!

1 2

P

1 2

p

p is for
pancakes

p is for
passion fruit

p is for
pepper

p is for
plum

TRY IT

1. Start with Bogart's emoji. Follow the lines.

P P P p p p

2. Try it out.

P p

Play the sound with the QR!

q is for
quail eggs

1. Start with Bogart's emoji. Follow the lines.

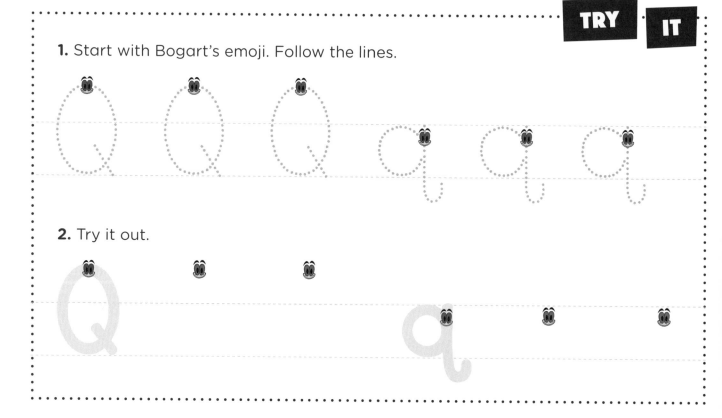

2. Try it out.

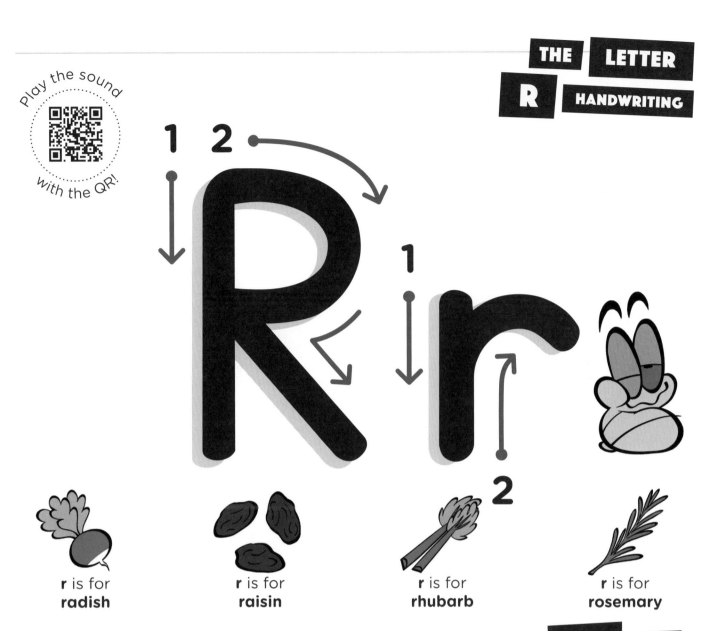

r is for
radish

r is for
raisin

r is for
rhubarb

r is for
rosemary

TRY IT

1. Start with Bogart's emoji. Follow the lines.

2. Try it out.

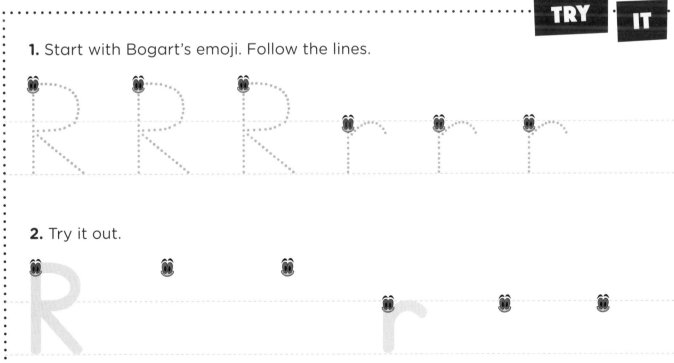

Play the sound with the QR!

s is for
salmon

s is for
slushie

s is for
squash

s is for
sweet potato

TRY IT

1. Start with Bogart's emoji. Follow the lines.

2. Try it out.

Play the sound with the QR!

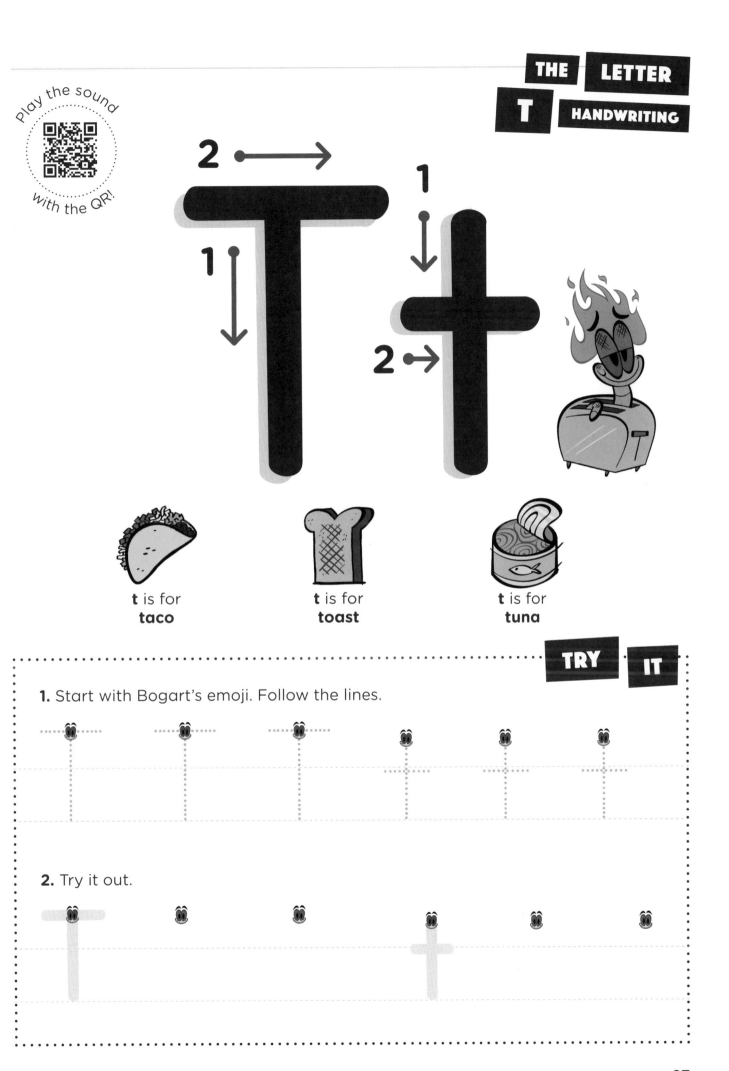

t is for
taco

t is for
toast

t is for
tuna

TRY IT

1. Start with Bogart's emoji. Follow the lines.

2. Try it out.

Play the sound with the QR!

u is for **umbrella**

TRY IT

1. Start with Bogart's emoji. Follow the lines.

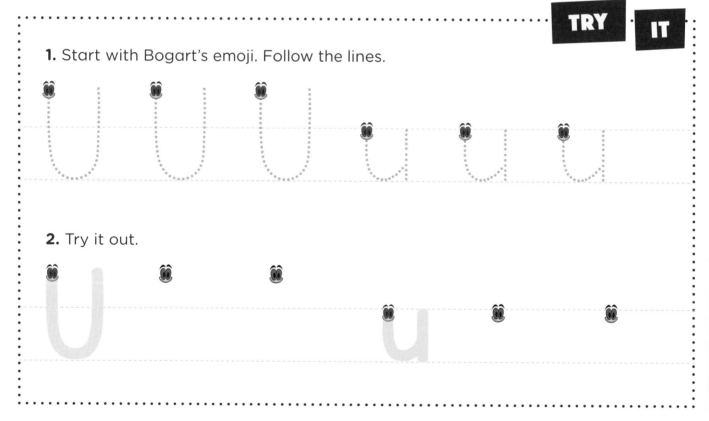

2. Try it out.

28

v is for
vinegar

TRY IT

1. Start with Bogart's emoji. Follow the lines.

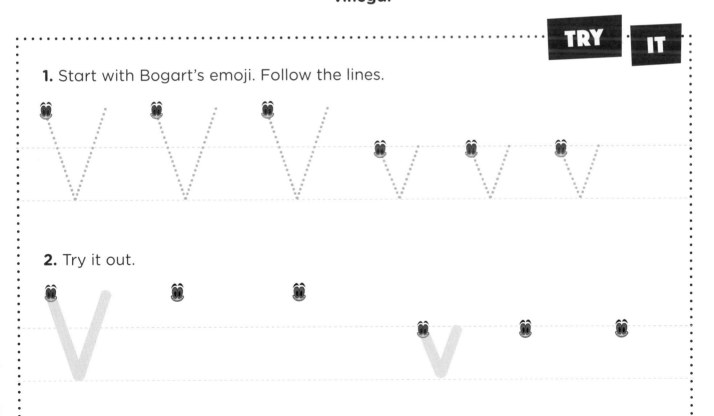

2. Try it out.

Play the sound with the QR!

w is for
walnuts

w is for
waffles

w is for
wasabi

w is for
watermelon

TRY IT

1. Start with Bogart's emoji. Follow the lines.

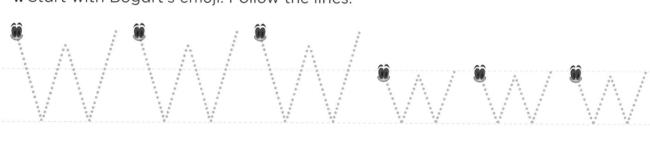

2. Try it out.

Play the sound with the QR!

x is for
e**x**tra lu**x**urious
Xmas cookies

TRY IT

1. Start with Bogart's emoji. Follow the lines.

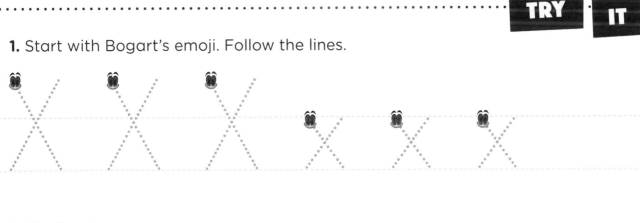

2. Try it out.

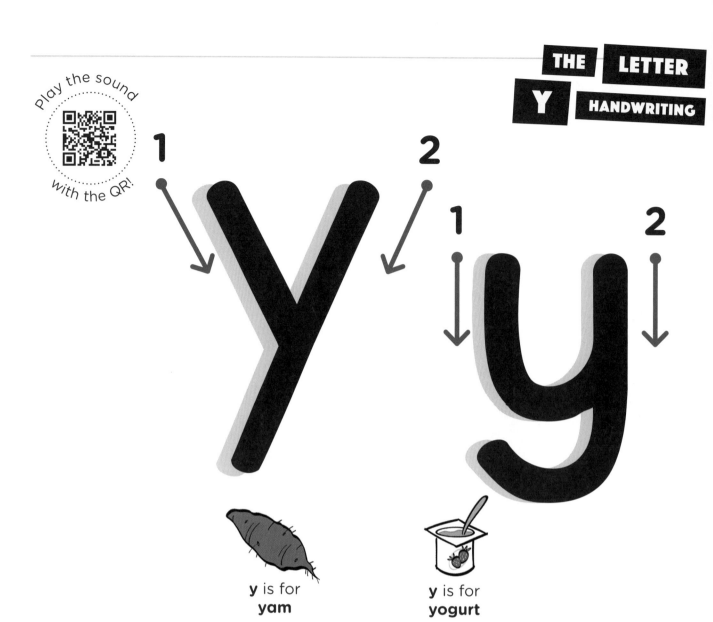

y is for **yam**

y is for **yogurt**

TRY IT

1. Start with Bogart's emoji. Follow the lines.

2. Try it out.

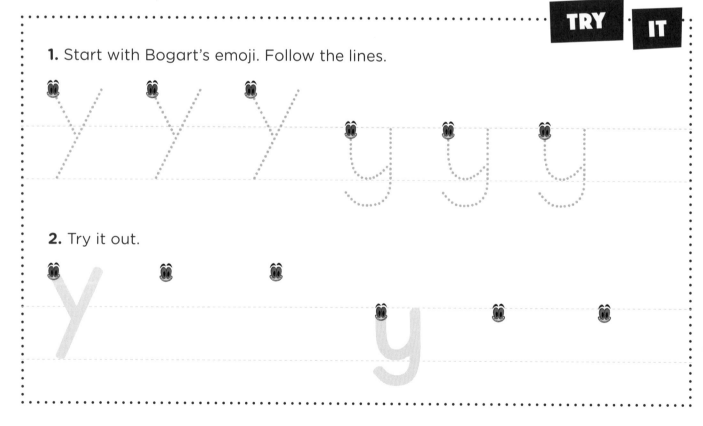

Play the sound with the QR!

z is for
zebra

TRY IT

1. Start with Bogart's emoji. Follow the lines.

2. Try it out.

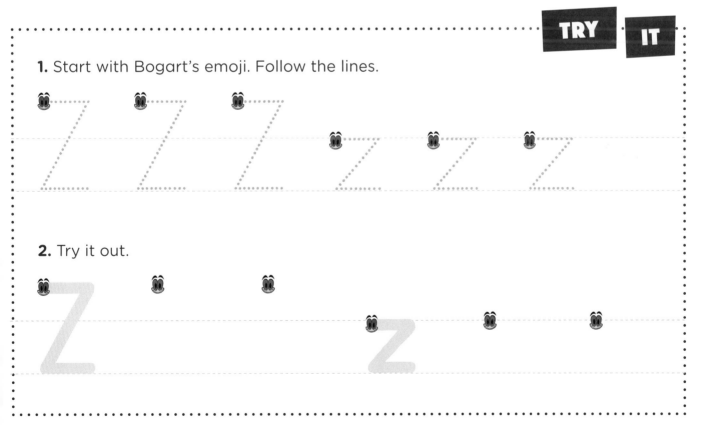

BOGART'S LOWER CASE ALPHABET

a b c d e f g

h i j k l m n

o p q r s t u

v w x y z

34

Trace the letters.

A B C D E F G

H I J K L M N

O P Q R S T U

V W X Y Z

Trace the letters.

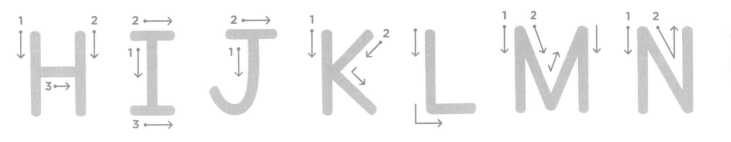

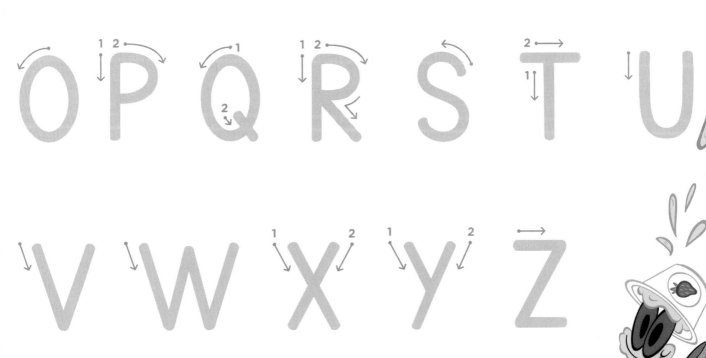

37

BOGART'S ALPHABET JUMBLE

Write the alphabet letters in the correct order.

Cross out each letter as you place it in order on the opposite page.

G F Q E C K

N Z M T L J

X A R D P I

H S W V U Y

B O

CONFUSING LETTERS:
b and d

Some letters look alike. Be careful when you read them and write them!
Use the word "bed" to remember the difference between b and d.

CONFUSING LETTERS:

p and q

Use the words "prince" and "queen" to remember
the difference between p and q.

CONFUSING LETTERS: LETTER PAINTING

1. Trace the letter.

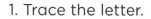

2. Try it out. Start with Bogart's emoji.

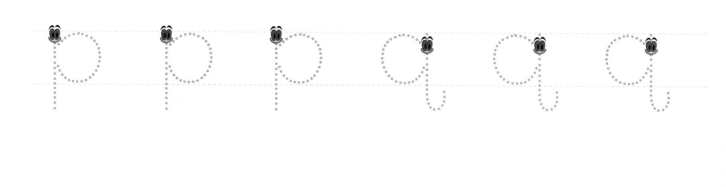

Try to spot the differences by colouring the letters like this:

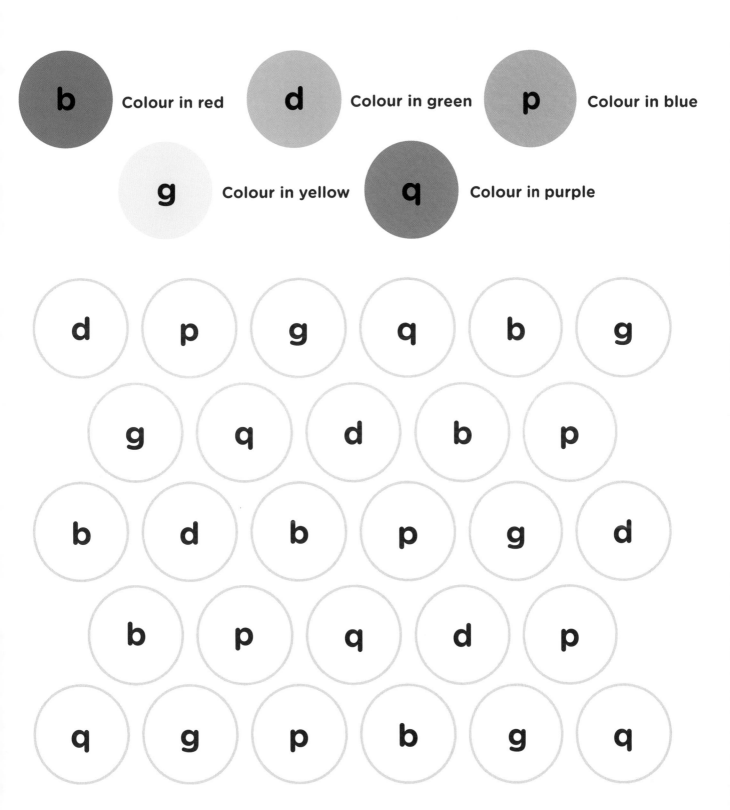

b Colour in red   d Colour in green   p Colour in blue

g Colour in yellow   q Colour in purple

d   p   g   q   b   g

g   q   d   b   p

b   d   b   p   g   d

b   p   q   d   p

q   g   p   b   g   q

PHONICS

PHONICS INSTRUCTIONS FOR GROWN-UPS

1

Say to your child, "This is the letter b." Scan the QR code with your mobile phone camera to hear the sound. Tell your child, "This is the sound the letter b makes. Can you copy this sound?" Repeat.

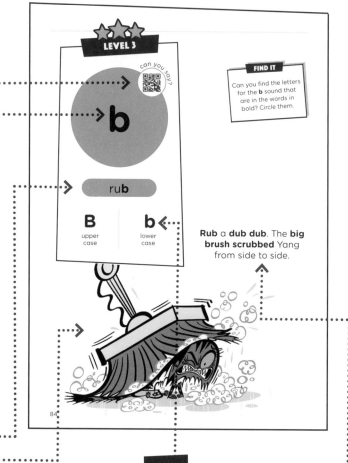

LEVEL 3

can you say?

b

ru**b**

B
upper case

b
lower case

FIND IT

Can you find the letters for the **b** sound that are in the words in bold? Circle them.

Rub a **dub dub**. The **big brush scrubbed** Yang from side to side.

2

Point to the letter several times and repeat the sound. This helps your child to pronounce the sound (phoneme) correctly, and link the phoneme with its written representation (grapheme).

3

Say the word slowly. Listen to how the sounds are blended together to make the word. Repeat the word with your child.

4

Tell your child that this letter can be written in two ways – upper case and lower case – depending on where it comes in a word or sentence. This can be quite confusing. When learning to read, we try to focus on the lower case letters first!

5

Look at the picture together and read the sentence to your child. Ask your child what is happening in the picture or what happens next? Remember, developing oral language and comprehension is also important when learning to read.

6

Point to the bold words in the sentence and ask your child to find all the "b" letters. The words with the "b" letters are emboldened to make it easier. They can't read these sentences yet. This is just to help them recognise what the letter looks like – and pick it out from a word. It may not be easy for them.

7

Read each sound slowly. The sound buttons under the letters tell you if the sounds are made up of one or more letters. In this image, "r-u-b" are all individual sounds. In other words, such as "care", the sound "are" is represented by three letters, but it is still a single sound. Ask your child to say the separate sounds slowly. Then say them again faster. Finally, blend the sounds together to make the word.

8

Trace the letter, first with a finger and then with a pencil. After your child has traced the letter three times, ask them to try writing the letter twice. This will really help them with handwriting later. When they have done this, practise reading the sounds and blending the word together again.

9

Here is a chance for your child to try writing the letter themselves. Starting at the correct point will really help. After they have traced the letter three times, ask them to try writing the letter twice. They should not worry if it doesn't look like the letter. It takes time to get this right.

10

These are words that your child can now try to read. With each word, they should first sound out the letters, then blend the sounds to read.

TRY IT

1. Read each sound. Read each sound again faster. Read the sounds together smoothly.

rub

2. Trace the dotted letter. Follow Bogart's emoji.

ru b

3. Trace and write the letters.

b b b _____

POWER UPS

Blend the letters to read the words.

big   bat   cab

85

can you say?

S

sat

S
upper case

s
lower case

FIND IT

Can you find the letters for the **s** sound that are in the words in bold? Circle them.

Bearnice **sat** on top of Brick. "Go **faster**!" she **said**.

48

1. Read each sound.
   Read each sound again
   faster. Read the sounds
   together smoothly.

2. Trace the dotted letter.
   Follow Bogart's emoji.

3. Trace and write the letters.

POWER UPS

Blend the letters
to read the words.

sit   sip

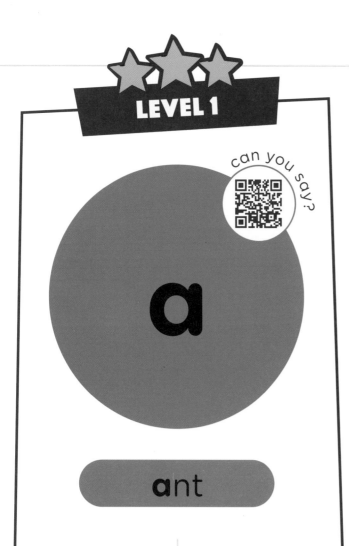

can you say?

a

ant

A	a
upper case	lower case

Barksy **had ants** in her **pants**.

1. Read each sound.
   Read each sound again
   faster. Read the sounds
   together smoothly.

2. Trace the dotted letter.
   Follow Bogart's emoji.

3. Trace and write the letters.

POWER UPS

Blend the letters
to read the words.

at   pan

can you say?

t

tap

T
upper case

t
lower case

FIND IT

Can you find the letters for the **t** sound that are in the words in bold? Circle them.

Turn on the **water tap**, **Grit**!

1. Read each sound.
   Read each sound again
   faster. Read the sounds
   together smoothly.

2. Trace the dotted letter.
   Follow Bogart's emoji.

3. Trace and write the letters.

POWER UPS

Blend the letters
to read the words.

tan   **tin**

can you say?

p

pat

P	p
upper case	lower case

Can you find the letters for the **p** sound that are in the words in bold? Circle them.

"Good **pup**!" said Bearnice. She likes to **pat** her **pup** on **top** of his head.

1. Read each sound.
   Read each sound again
   faster. Read the sounds
   together smoothly.

2. Trace the dotted letter.
   Follow Bogart's emoji.

3. Trace and write the letters.

POWER UPS

Blend the letters
to read the words.

nip   **tip**

can you say?

i

sip

I	**i**
upper case	lower case

Can you find the letters for the **i** sound that are in the words in bold? Circle them.

Oz sat on the sofa and **sipped** a hot **drink**.

1. Read each sound.
   Read each sound again
   faster. Read the sounds
   together smoothly.

2. Trace the dotted letter.
   Follow Bogart's emoji.

3. Trace and write the letters.

POWER UPS

Blend the letters
to read the words.

nip   **tip**

can you say?

nap

N
upper case

n
lower case

FIND IT

Can you find the letters for the **n** sound that are in the words in bold? Circle them.

Brick had a **nap under** the tree.

1. Read each sound.
   Read each sound again
   faster. Read the sounds
   together smoothly.

2. Trace the dotted letter.
   Follow Bogart's emoji.

3. Trace and write the letters.

POWER UPS

Blend the letters
to read the words.

an   pin

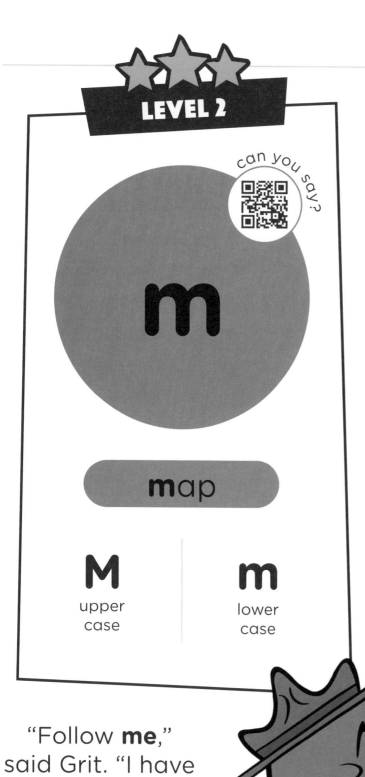

LEVEL 2

can you say?

m

map

M
upper case

m
lower case

FIND IT

Can you find the letters for the **m** sound that are in the words in bold? Circle them.

"Follow **me**," said Grit. "I have a **map**."

1. Read each sound.
   Read each sound again
   faster. Read the sounds
   together smoothly.

2. Trace the dotted letter.
   Follow Bogart's emoji.

3. Trace and write the letters.

POWER UPS

Blend the letters
to read the words.

man   **mat**

can you say?

d

sa**d**

D	**d**
upper case	lower case

FIND IT

Can you find the letters for the **d** sound that are in the words in bold? Circle them.

Bogart felt **sad today**. It was **drizzling outside**.

1. Read each sound.
   Read each sound again
   faster. Read the sounds
   together smoothly.

2. Trace the dotted letter.
   Follow Bogart's emoji.

3. Trace and write the letters.

POWER UPS

Blend the letters
to read the words.

mad   dam   dip

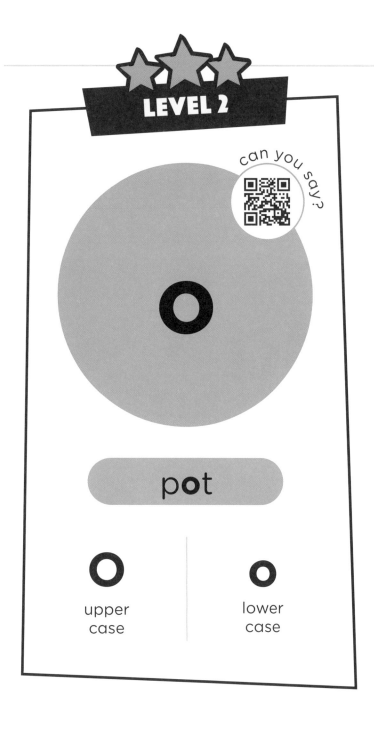

can you say?

pot

O
upper case

O
lower case

FIND IT

Can you find the letters for the **o** sound that are in the words in bold? Circle them.

The **pot on** the table is empty.

1. Read each sound.
   Read each sound again
   faster. Read the sounds
   together smoothly.

2. Trace the dotted letter.
   Follow Bogart's emoji.

3. Trace and write the letters.

POWER UPS

Blend the letters
to read the words.

on   top   hot

can you say?

g

dog

G
upper case

g
lower case

Can you find the letters for the **g** sound that are in the words in bold? Circle them.

Grit the **dog** chased his tail.

1. Read each sound. Read each sound again faster. Read the sounds together smoothly.

2. Trace the dotted letter. Follow Bogart's emoji.

3. Trace and write the letters.

POWER UPS

Blend the letters to read the words.

dig tag gas

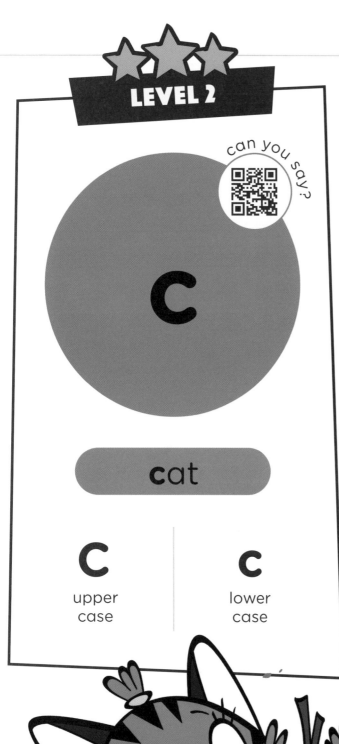

can you say?

c

cat

C
upper case

c
lower case

Can you find the letters for the **c** sound that are in the words in bold? Circle them.

The **cats** drew a **cool picture** in the sand.

1. Read each sound.
   Read each sound again
   faster. Read the sounds
   together smoothly.

2. Trace the dotted letter.
   Follow Bogart's emoji.

3. Trace and write the letters.

POWER UPS

Blend the letters
to read the words.

can cap cot

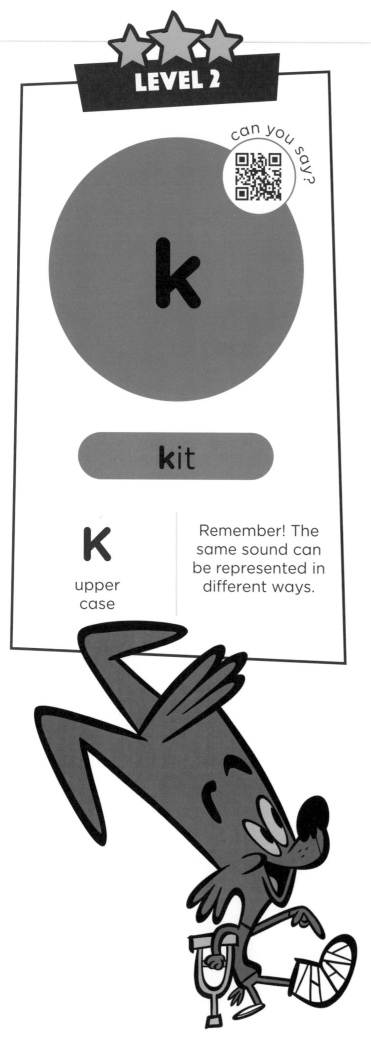

can you say?

k

kit

K

upper case

Remember! The same sound can be represented in different ways.

FIND IT

Can you find the letters for the **k** sound that are in the words in bold? Circle them.

"Do you have a first aid **kit** for **kids**?" Grit **asked**.

1. Read each sound. Read each sound again faster. Read the sounds together smoothly.

kit

2. Trace the dotted letter. Follow Bogart's emoji.

3. Trace and write the letters.

POWER UPS

Blend the letters to read the words.

kin   **kid**

can you say?

ck

kick

CK
upper case

Remember! A single sound can be represented by two letters.

FIND IT

Can you find the letters for the **ck** sound that are in the words in bold? Circle them.

Bearnice **kicked** the ball into the sky.

Thwack!

72

TRY IT

1. Read each sound. Read each sound again faster. Read the sounds together smoothly.

2. Trace the dotted letter. Follow Bogart's emoji.

3. Trace and write the letters.

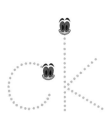

POWER UPS

Blend the letters to read the words.

pick sick sock

Practise the words you learned in Level 2.

map	on
man	top
mat	can
sad	cap
mad	cot
dam	kit
dip	kin
dog	kid
dig	
tag	
gas	
pot	

You've got this!

Try these harder words with consonant clusters (two or more consonants side by side). You can do it! You have learned all the sounds.

You can do it!

mint

damp

sand

gap

pig

stop

act

camp

skin

snack

stick

can you say?

e

net

E
upper case

e
lower case

FIND IT

Can you find the letters for the **e** sound that are in the words in bold? Circle them.

Let's use a **net** to catch a **yellow** star!

1. Read each sound. Read each sound again faster. Read the sounds together smoothly.

2. Trace the dotted letter. Follow Bogart's emoji.

3. Trace and write the letters.

POWER UPS

Blend the letters to read the words.

ten   met   get

can you say?

u

mud

U
upper case

u
lower case

Yin **jumped up** and down in the **mud**.

78

1. Read each sound.
   Read each sound again
   faster. Read the sounds
   together smoothly.

2. Trace the dotted letter.
   Follow Bogart's emoji.

3. Trace and write the letters.

POWER UPS

Blend the letters
to read the words.

cut nut sun

can you say?

r

rock

R	r
upper case	lower case

Can you find the letters for the **r** sound that are in the words in bold? Circle them.

Shang High **dropped** the **rock right** on his big toe!

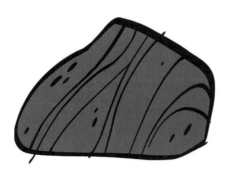

rock

1. Read each sound. Read each sound again faster. Read the sounds together smoothly.

2. Trace the dotted letter. Follow Bogart's emoji.

3. Trace and write the letters.

POWER UPS

Blend the letters to read the words.

run   red   rat

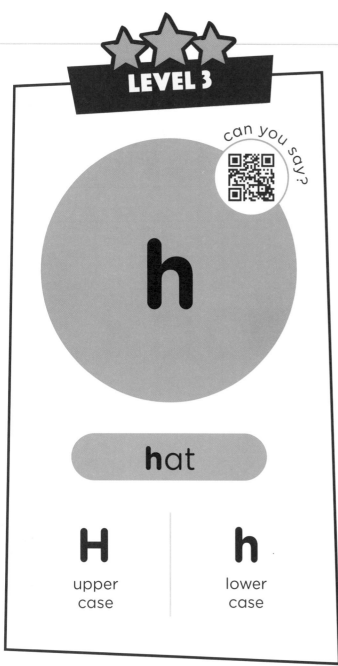

can you say?

h

hat

H	h
upper case	lower case

Can you find the letters for the **h** sound that are in the words in bold? Circle them.

Plato is wearing a **huge hat** on **his head**.

1. Read each sound.
   Read each sound again
   faster. Read the sounds
   together smoothly.

2. Trace the dotted letter.
   Follow Bogart's emoji.

3. Trace and write the letters.

POWER UPS

Blend the letters
to read the words.

hug   him   hit

83

can you say?

b

rub

B
upper case

b
lower case

Rub a **dub dub**. The **big brush scrubbed** Yang from side to side.

1. Read each sound.
   Read each sound again
   faster. Read the sounds
   together smoothly.

2. Trace the dotted letter.
   Follow Bogart's emoji.

3. Trace and write the letters.

POWER UPS

Blend the letters
to read the words.

big   bat   cab

can you say?

f

fib

F
upper case

f
lower case

Can you find the letters for the **f** sound that are in the words in bold? Circle them.

Armie told a **fib** about a **fight** with a big **fish**.

fib

1. Read each sound.
   Read each sound again
   faster. Read the sounds
   together smoothly.

2. Trace the dotted letter.
   Follow Bogart's emoji.

3. Trace and write the letters.

POWER UPS

Blend the letters
to read the words.

fun   fit   fed

can you say?

ff

puff

FF
upper case

Remember! A single sound can be represented by two letters.

Can you find the letters for the **ff** sound that are in the words in bold? Circle them.

The **giraffe huffed** and **puffed** until he blew out all the candles.

1. Read each sound.
   Read each sound again
   faster. Read the sounds
   together smoothly.

2. Trace the dotted letter.
   Follow Bogart's emoji.

3. Trace and write the letters.

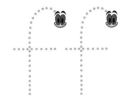

POWER UPS

Blend the letters
to read the words.

off   huff   sniff

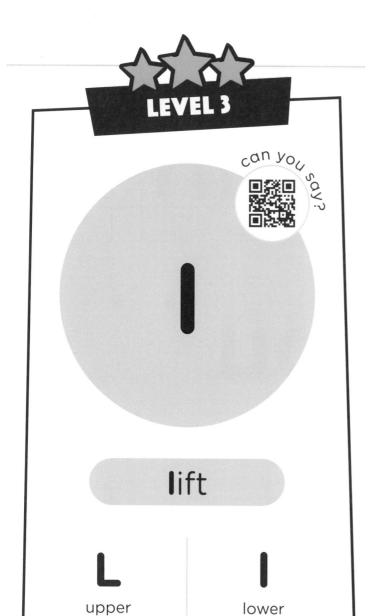

can you say?

l

lift

L
upper case

I
lower case

Can you find the letters for the **l** sound that are in the words in bold? Circle them.

Shang High **lifted** the rock and found a **little** worm.

"Hi Bogart!"

TRY IT

lift

1. Read each sound.
   Read each sound again
   faster. Read the sounds
   together smoothly.

ift

2. Trace the dotted letter.
   Follow Bogart's emoji.

3. Trace and write the letters.

POWER UPS

Blend the letters
to read the words.

lip   lot   leg

91

can you say?

ll

smell

LL
upper case

ll
lower case

Can you find the letters for the **ll** sound that are in the words in bold? Circle them.

Brick **fell** in love with the **smell** of **all** the flowers.

1. Read each sound.
   Read each sound again
   faster. Read the sounds
   together smoothly.

smell

2. Trace the dotted letter.
   Follow Bogart's emoji.

smell

3. Trace and write the letters.

POWER UPS

Blend the letters
to read the words.

tell pill bell

can you say?

SS

me**ss**

SS
upper case

ss
lower case

Can you find the letters for the **ss** sound that are in the words in bold? Circle them.

Grit was very **stressed** about cleaning up his **mess**.

1. Read each sound.
   Read each sound again
   faster. Read the sounds
   together smoothly.

mess

2. Trace the dotted letter.
   Follow Bogart's emoji.

me

3. Trace and write the letters.

POWER UPS

Blend the letters
to read the words.

kiss   less   boss

Practise the words you learned in Level 3.

You've got this!

rat

hug

ten

get

hit

met

him

cut

big

nut

bat

sun

cab

run

fun

red

fit

fed

Try these harder words with consonant clusters (two or more consonants side by side). You can do it! You have learned all the sounds.

tent

bed

bend

rest

mug

truck

hand

bus

bad

best

muffin

left

help

luck

sell

You can do it!

can you say?

j

jump

J
upper case

j
lower case

Oz **jumped** for **joy**. She **just** felt so happy.

1. Read each sound.
   Read each sound again
   faster. Read the sounds
   together smoothly.

2. Trace the dotted letter.
   Follow Bogart's emoji.

3. Trace and write the letters.

POWER UPS

Blend the letters
to read the words.

jog   jam   jet

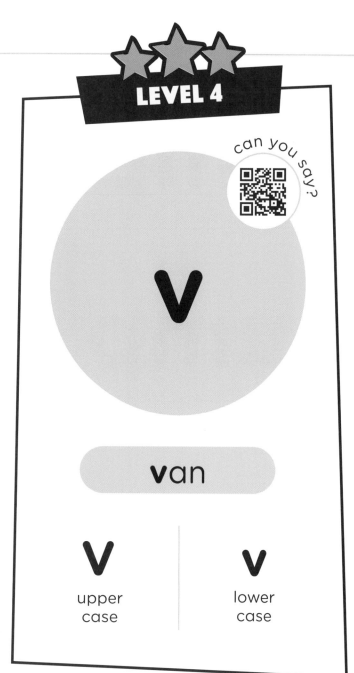

can you say?

van

V
upper case

v
lower case

Can you find the letters for the **v** sound that are in the words in bold? Circle them.

Vroom! Vroom! The noisy **van drove** away **very** quickly.

1. Read each sound. Read each sound again faster. Read the sounds together smoothly.

2. Trace the dotted letter. Follow Bogart's emoji.

3. Trace and write the letters.

POWER UPS

Blend the letters to read the words.

vet   vat

can you say?

w

wet

W
upper case

w
lower case

Grit sprayed **water** on Plato's face.

Plato did not **want** to get **wet**!

wet

1. Read each sound.
   Read each sound again
   faster. Read the sounds
   together smoothly.

2. Trace the dotted letter.
   Follow Bogart's emoji.

3. Trace and write the letters.

POWER UPS

Blend the letters
to read the words.

will   **web**

can you say?

x

fix

X
upper case

X
lower case

"Relax," said Yin.

"We can **fix** it! All we need is some **extra**-strong glue."

fix

1. Read each sound.
Read each sound again
faster. Read the sounds
together smoothly.

2. Trace the dotted letter.
Follow Bogart's emoji.

3. Trace and write the letters.

POWER UPS

Blend the letters
to read the words.

box   fox   six

can you say?

y

yell

Y	y
upper case	lower case

FIND IT

Can you find the letters for the **y** sound that are in the words in bold? Circle them.

"**Yes**, okay! **You** don't need to shout!" Plato said.

Grit should not **yell** at Plato.

1. Read each sound.
   Read each sound again
   faster. Read the sounds
   together smoothly.

2. Trace the dotted letter.
   Follow Bogart's emoji.

3. Trace and write the letters.

POWER UPS

Blend the letters
to read the words.

yes   yap

can you say?

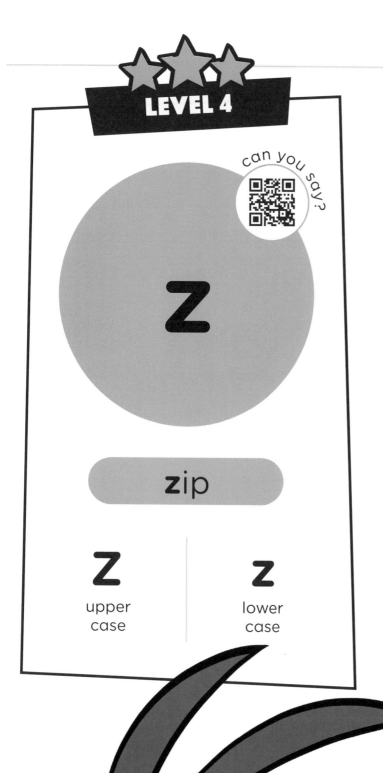

z

zip

Z
upper case

z
lower case

Can you find the letters for the **z** sound that are in the words in bold? Circle them.

"Your mouth is **zipped**!" cried Armie.
"I will **unzip** it!"

1. Read each sound.
   Read each sound again
   faster. Read the sounds
   together smoothly.

2. Trace the dotted letter.
   Follow Bogart's emoji.

3. Trace and write the letters.

POWER UPS

Blend the letters
to read the words.

zap   **zigzag**

can you say?

zz

bu**zz**

ZZ
upper case

zz
lower case

The bees **buzzed** as they **whizzed** through **dazzling** sunshine.

110

1. Read each sound.
   Read each sound again
   faster. Read the sounds
   together smoothly.

2. Trace the dotted letter.
   Follow Bogart's emoji.

3. Trace and write the letters.

POWER UPS

Blend the letters
to read the words.

fizz   fuzz   jazz

can you say?

sh

flush

SH
upper case

sh
lower case

Can you find the letters for the **sh** sound that are in the words in bold? Circle them.

"Don't forget to **flush** the toilet!" **shouted** Oz.

"**Shoo shoo**, little poo!"

flush

1. Read each sound.
   Read each sound again
   faster. Read the sounds
   together smoothly.

2. Trace the dotted letter.
   Follow Bogart's emoji.

3. Trace and write the letters.

POWER UPS

Blend the letters
to read the words.

fish   wish   shop

can you say?

ch

chat

CH
upper case

ch
lower case

FIND IT

Can you find the letters for the **ch** sound that are in the words in bold? Circle them.

"**Cheer** up!" **chuckled** Plato.

"We can **chat** on the phone until you feel better."

1. Read each sound.
   Read each sound again
   faster. Read the sounds
   together smoothly.

2. Trace the dotted letter.
   Follow Bogart's emoji.

3. Trace and write the letters.

POWER UPS

Blend the letters
to read the words.

chop   chin   rich

can you say?

th

thick

TH	**th**
upper case	lower case

FIND IT

Can you find the letters for the **th** sound that are in the words in bold? Circle them.

Yang drew a **thin** line

and Yin drew a **thick** line.

116

1. Read each sound.
   Read each sound again
   faster. Read the sounds
   together smoothly.

2. Trace the dotted letter.
   Follow Bogart's emoji.

3. Trace and write the letters.

POWER UPS

Blend the letters
to read the words.

moth   thin   cloth

CVC a
BUBBLE BATH

Can you make three CVC (consonant vowel consonant) words like "c-a-t"? Choose a beginning consonant and an ending consonant and write them in the CVC bubbles. Draw some more bubbles and make more CVC words!

BEGINNING CONSONANTS

b c d
f g h
j l m
n p r
s t v
w y

a

a

a

ENDING CONSONANTS

b d g
m n p
t

118

cvc e
BUBBLE BATH

e

e

e

BEGINNING CONSONANTS

b d f
g h j
l m n
p r s
t v w
y

ENDING CONSONANTS

d g n
t

119

CVC i
BUBBLE BATH

Can you make three CVC (consonant vowel consonant) words like "s-i-t"? Choose a beginning consonant and an ending consonant and write them in the CVC bubbles. Draw some more bubbles and make more CVC words!

BEGINNING CONSONANTS

b d f

g h j

k l m

n p r

s t v

w y z

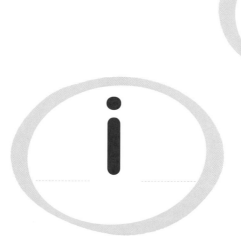

ENDING CONSONANTS

d g m

n p t

CVC O
BUBBLE BATH

O

O

O

b c d
f g h
j l m
n p r
s t

b g m
p t x

CVC U
BUBBLE BATH

Can you make three CVC (consonant vowel consonant) words like "s-u-n"? Choose a beginning consonant and an ending consonant and write them in the CVC bubbles. Draw some more bubbles and make more CVC words!

BEGINNING CONSONANTS

b c d
f g h
j l m
n p r
s t

ENDING CONSONANTS

b d g
m n p
t s

122

When two letters come together to make one sound, they are called a **digraph**.

Some words end with the double letters "**ss**", "**ll**", "**ff**", "**zz**", "**ck**".

Circle the word that matches the picture.

1. (kiss)   puff

2. fill   bell

3. buzz   sniff

4. duck   sell

5. mess   back

6. dress   less

SHORT VOWELS: COMPLETE THE WORDS

Complete these words with the correct short vowel to make a real word.

1. c a t

2. j mp

3. h nd

4. b ck

5. w sh

VOWELS

(a)	i
e	u
o	a
a	o
u	i

Vowel sounds can be long or short.

The sound of **a** in **apple** is a short vowel sound.
The sound of **ai** in **rain** is a long vowel sound.

6. r ___ d

7. b ___ x

8. f ___ sh

9. ___ g g

10. b ___ s

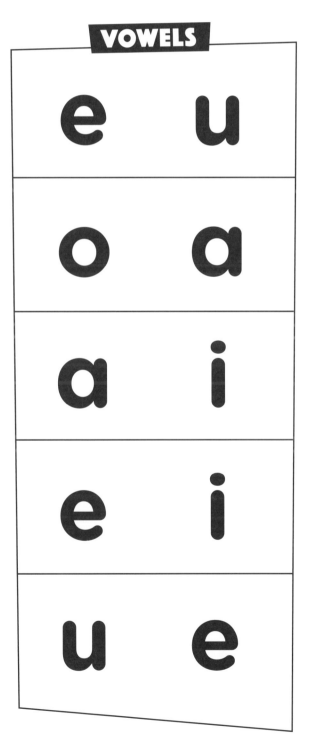

VOWELS

e	u
o	a
a	i
e	i
u	e

INSTRUCTIONS:

1. Sound button the words.

When a single letter (grapheme) makes one sound (phoneme), put a **dot** under it.

cat
. . .

2. Blend and read the words.

1.	**cat**	2.	**run**
3.	**gap**	4.	**mop**
5.	**fun**	6.	**sit**
7.	**pot**	8.	**net**
9.	**wig**	10.	**fox**

11. **sad**   12. **hat**

13. **wet**   14. **mud**

15. **lip**   16. **dog**

17. **zip**   18. **box**

Try to decode these non-real words in the same way.

19. **bab**   20. **gab**

21. **beb**   22. **cag**

127

PHONICS:
SOUND BUTTONS &
READING PRACTICE

INSTRUCTIONS:

1. Sound button the words.

   When a single letter (grapheme) makes one sound (phoneme), put a **dot** under it.

   cat
   • • •

2. Blend and read the words.

3. Real or not real?

   On this page there are words that are real and words that are not real. You have to decide which is which.

   Tick the box if the word is **real**.

   cat ✓   pag ☐
   • • •   • • •

1. **pin** ☐   2. **dim** ☐

3. **hig** ☐   4. **fim** ☐

5. **mub** ☐   6. **bet** ☐

7. **tin** ☐   8. **men** ☐

9. **beg** ☐   10. **mab** ☐

11. **gel** ☐   12. **mup** ☐

13. **yes** ☐   14. **jub** ☐

15. **leg** ☐   16. **six** ☐

17. **tap** ☐   18. **dat** ☐

19. **mit** ☐   20. **bag** ☐

1. Sound button the words.

When a single letter (grapheme) makes one sound (phoneme), put a **dot** under it.

cat
• • •

Spot the digraphs (two letters that make one sound) and **underline** them.

chat
— • •

2. Blend and read the words.

1.	**buzz**	2.	**back**
3.	**luck**	4.	**chat**
5.	**tell**	6.	**rich**
7.	**pick**	8.	**shop**

Level 2: CVC words with consonant digraphs and short vowels.

9.	**ship**	10.	**miss**
11.	**puff**	12.	**chop**
13.	**that**	14.	**with**
15.	**much**	16.	**sack**

Try to decode these non-real words in the same way.

17.	**pezz**	18.	**yich**
19.	**kaff**	20.	**tezz**

PHONICS:
SOUND BUTTONS &
READING PRACTICE

1. Sound button the words.

When a single letter (grapheme) makes one sound (phoneme), put a **dot** under it.

cat
• • •

Spot the digraphs (two letters that make one sound) and **underline** them.

chat
— • •

2. Blend and read the words.

3. Real or not real?

On this page there are words that are real and words that are not real. You have to decide which is which.

Tick the box if the word is **real**.

cat ✓   **pag** ☐
• • •   • • •

1. **hill** ☐   2. **bell** ☐

3. **yell** ☐   4. **kezz** ☐

5. **well** ☐   6. **check** ☐

7. **dull** ☐   8. **moth** ☐

Level 2: CVC words with consonant digraphs and short vowels.

9. **jazz** ☐

10. **chill** ☐

11. **juck** ☐

12. **zoth** ☐

13. **coss** ☐

14. **shup** ☐

15. **chuck** ☐

16. **rell** ☐

17. **fizz** ☐

18. **bill** ☐

19. **rock** ☐

20. **shut** ☐

VOCABULARY

big

larger than normal

Circle the word that means the opposite of big.

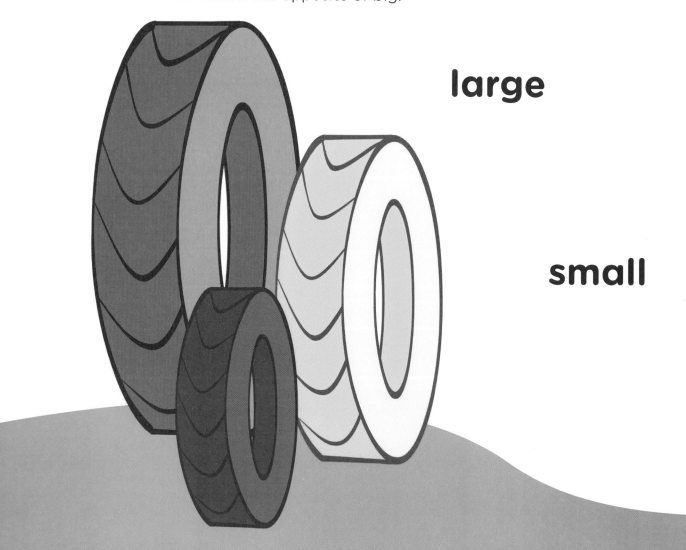

large

small

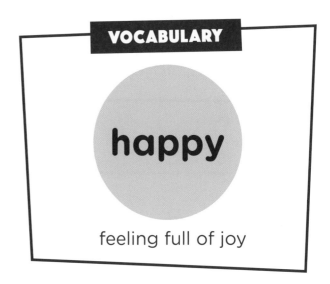

VOCABULARY

happy

feeling full of joy

Circle the word that means the opposite of happy.

sad

cheerful

Prepositions tell you where something is
or where something happens.

Write the prepositions next to the matching picture.

1.

on

2.   3.

beneath | **in** | **on**

4.

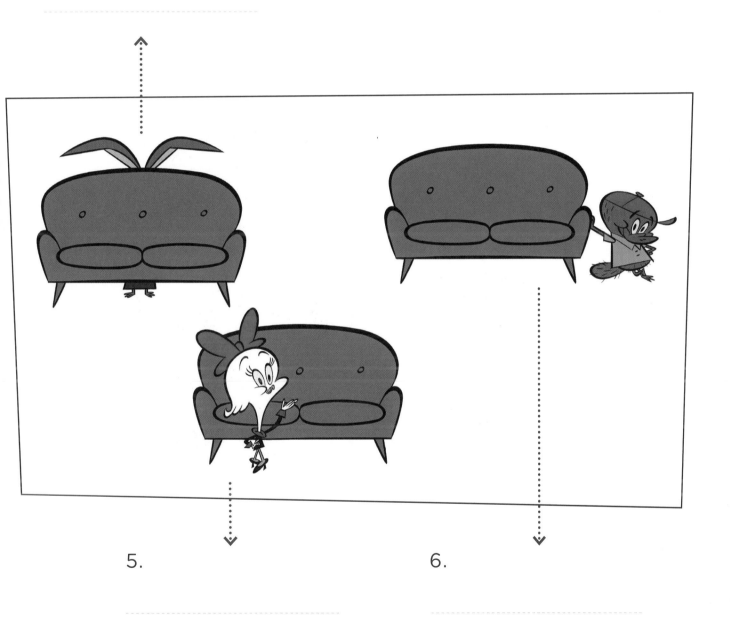

5.

6.

in front of | **next to** | **behind**

Cause and effect show how two events are related.
The second event (effect) happens as a
result of the first event (cause).

CAUSE:

What happened first?

Draw what you think will happen as a result of the first image.

What happened as a result?

CAUSE & EFFECT

Draw what you think happened first.

CAUSE:

What happened first?

Cause and effect show how two events are related.
The second event (effect) happens as a
result of the first event (cause).

What happened as a result?

CAUSE
& EFFECT

Draw what you think happened first.

CAUSE:

What happened first?

Cause and effect show how two events are related.
The second event (effect) happens as a
result of the first event (cause).

EFFECT:

What happened as a result?

Write **1** in the circle to show what happened **first**.
Write **2** in the circle to show what happened **next**.
Write **3** in the circle to show what happened **last**.

Can you retell this story?

SORT OBJECTS INTO CATEGORIES

Circle all the fruits.

Help me choose a healthy snack!

Circle all the cars.

Which flowers are different, and which are the same?

Circle the flowers that are the same.

WHICH FEELING MATCHES THE EMOJI?

Draw a line from the emoji to the matching emotion.

| sad | laughing | angry | happy | crying |

1.

2.

3.

4.

5.

HIGH-FREQUENCY WORDS

HIGH-FREQUENCY WORDS

Use the paint-by-words chart to complete the picture. Use crayons, pencils, or paint!

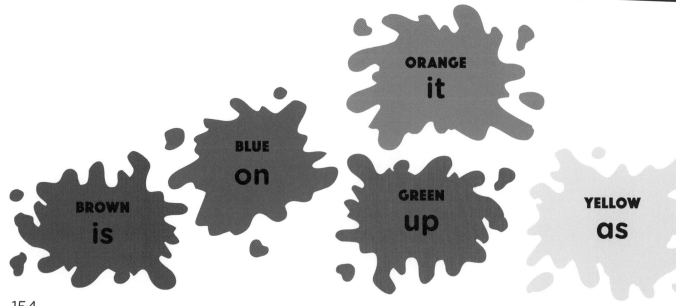

ORANGE
it

BLUE
on

BROWN
is

GREEN
up

YELLOW
as

Use the paint by words chart to complete the picture and find the hidden words. Use crayons, pencils, or paint!

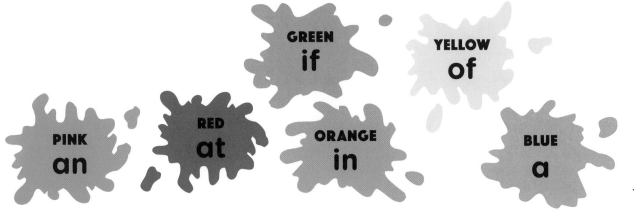

GREEN if

YELLOW of

PINK an

RED at

ORANGE in

BLUE a

HIGH-FREQUENCY WORDS

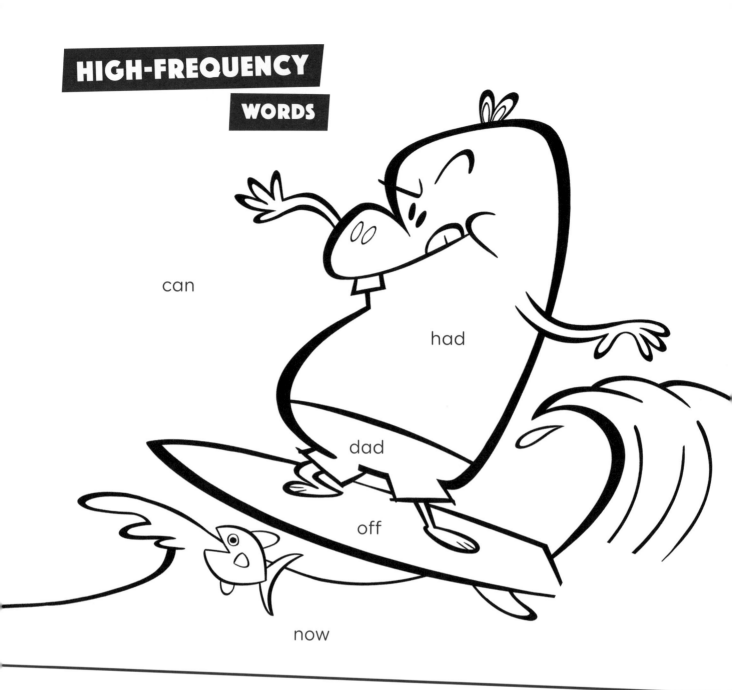

can

had

dad

off

now

Use the paint by words chart to complete the picture. Use crayons, pencils, or paint!

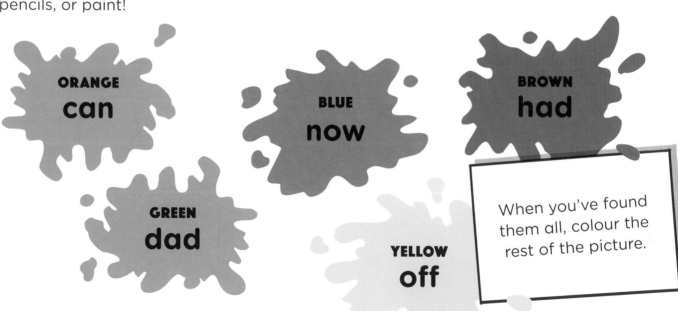

ORANGE
can

BLUE
now

BROWN
had

GREEN
dad

YELLOW
off

When you've found them all, colour the rest of the picture.

Trace the dotted letters.

off

can

dad

had

now

Use the paint by words chart to complete the picture and find the hidden words. Use crayons, pencils, or paint!

PURPLE to

YELLOW but

RED mum

ORANGE I

BROWN got

BLUE no

Trace the dotted letters.

got

mum

but

MATHS CONCEPTS & VOCABULARY

COUNTING SHEEP

Help Shang High fall asleep by counting the sheep. Choose the correct number to write in the gaps.

I can't sleep!

CHOOSE HERE

1   8   10   7   9   6   2   5   3   4

- - - - - - - - - -

- - - - - - - - - -

- - - - - - - - - -

- - - - - - - - - -

COUNT WITH SHANG HIGH

Shang High is planning his birthday party! Count the items and choose the correct number to write in each gap.

CHOOSE HERE

1   2   3   4   5   6   7   8   9   10

1.

3

2.

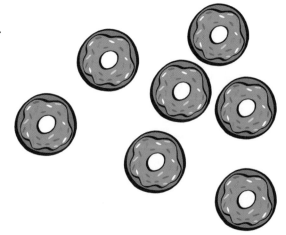

3.

4.

5.

6.

7.

8.

Count the number of cookies in these groups. Choose the correct number to write in each gap.

CHOOSE **HERE**

1 2 3 4 5 6 7 8 9 10

1.

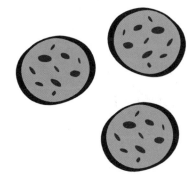

3

2.

3.

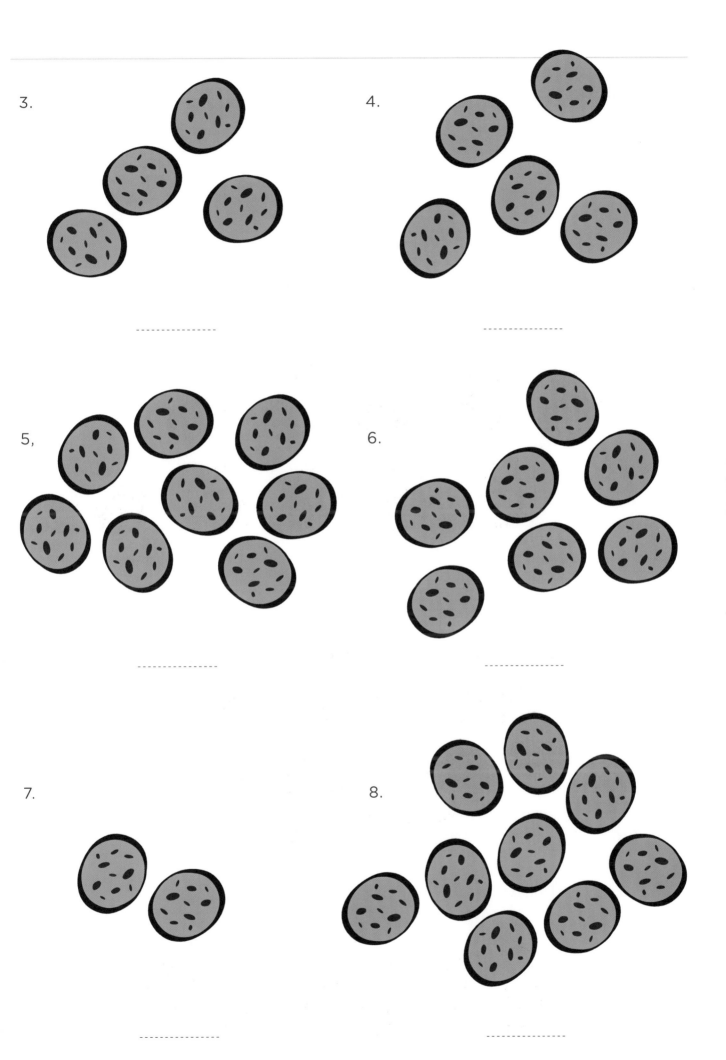

4.

5.

6.

7.

8.

COUNTING GROUPS OF ANIMALS

Count the number of animals in each group.

CHOOSE HERE

1 2 3 4 5 6 7 8 9 10

1. There are _____ bees in this swarm.

2. There are _____ cows in this herd.

3. There are _____ sheep in this flock.

168

4. There are _____ fish in this school.

5. There are _____ ants in this colony.

6. There are _____ wolves in this pack.

WHICH HAS MORE?

Circle the group that has more.

1.

 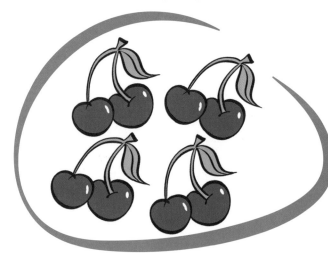

2.

3.

4.

Circle the group that has fewer.

1.

 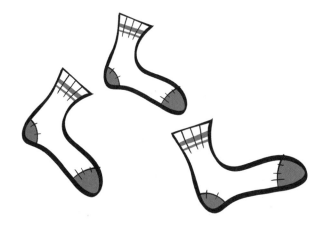

2.

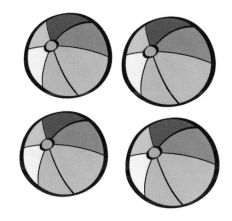 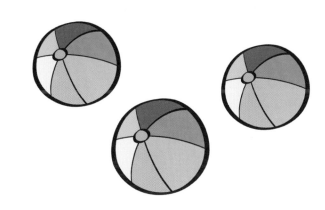

3.

4.

COMPARING SIZES

Circle which is bigger.

Circle which is smaller.

Circle who is shorter.

Circle which is taller.

Circle which is lighter.

Circle who is heavier.

173

Continue the pattern by
colouring in the white circles.

1.

2.

3.

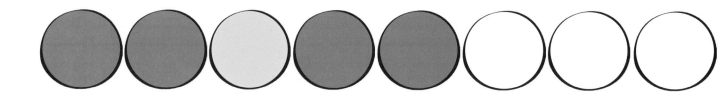

4.

5.

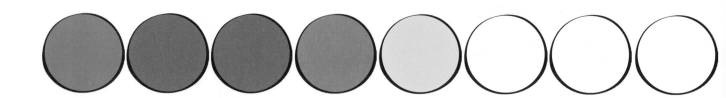

Fill in the missing pattern by
colouring in the white circles.

1.

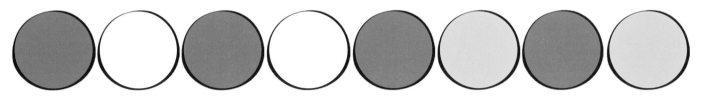

2.

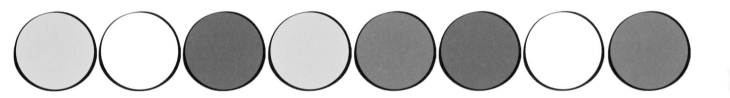

3.

4.

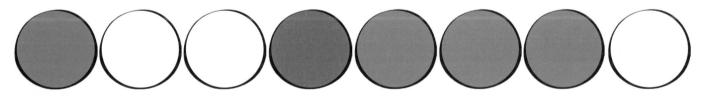

5.

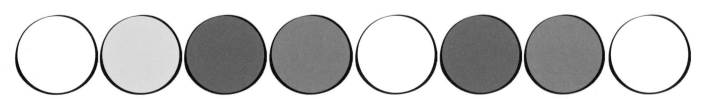

NUMBER BONDS

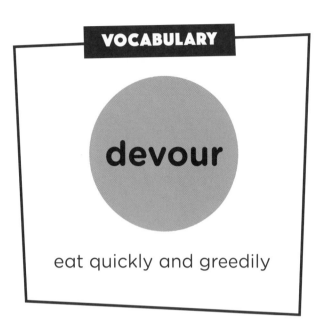

devour

eat quickly and greedily

PIE EATING CONTEST

Use the stack of pies (or your fingers) to help you complete the number bonds.

1. **1** + 9 = **10**

2. **2** + ___ = **10**

3.  **3** + ___ = **10**

4.  **4** + ___ = **10**

5.  **5** + ___ = **10**

2D SHAPES

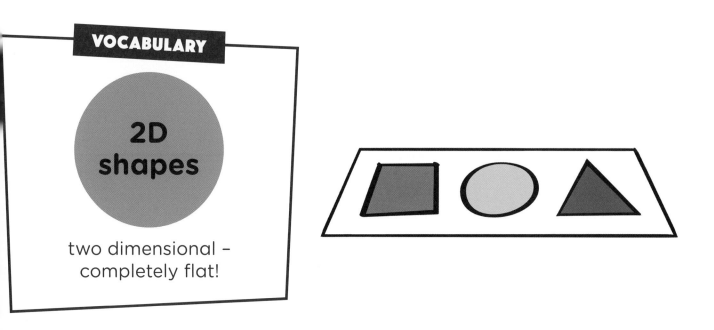

Draw a line with your pencil and match each shape to its name.

square

circle

oval

pentagon

triangle

hexagon

heptagon

rectangle

octagon

rhombus

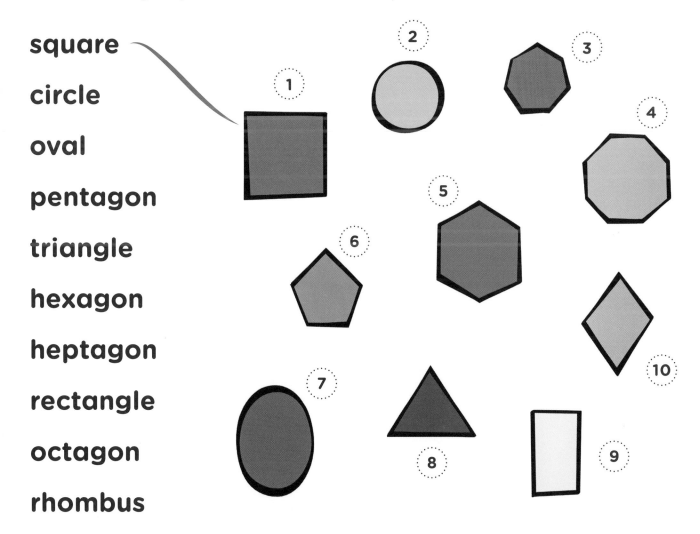

LISTENING, SPEAKING, CREATING

Shang High is listening with his whole body

Eyes
Look at the person talking to you

Brain
Awake and thinking about what is being said

Mouth
Quiet! No talking, humming, or making sounds

Ears
Ready to hear

Heart
Caring about what the other person is saying

Body
Facing the speaker

Feet
Still on the floor

Hands
Still on your lap or by your sides

THIS IS MY FAMILY

**HI!
MY NAME IS**

_____

Draw your
me-moji:

I AM

_____

**YEARS
OLD**

Circle a me-moji
that shows how
you feel.

MY FRIENDS ARE:

 _____

 _____

 _____

 _____

HAPPY

SILLY

SAD

CONFUSED

MISCHIEVOUS

Teddy Talks are about creating something new and sharing it with the world!

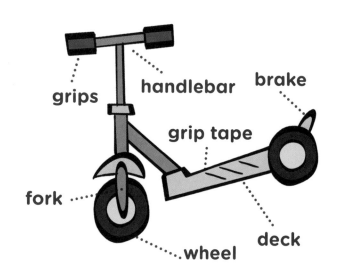

grips

handlebar

brake

grip tape

fork

wheel

deck

VOCABULARY

scooter

a vehicle with two wheels

Design your own scooter on the next page.
Use some of ours for inspiration!

Scooter of the future

DESIGN ON NEXT PAGE

Design your own scooter here.

TEDDY Talks DESIGN YOUR OWN DRONE

Teddy Talks are about creating something new and sharing it with the world!

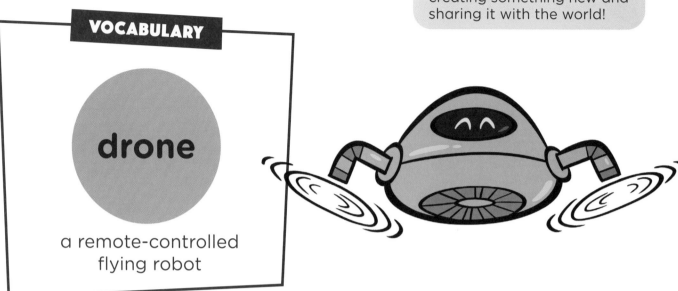

drone

a remote-controlled flying robot

Design your own drone on the next page.
Don't forget to give it a name!
These are parts used to make a drone.

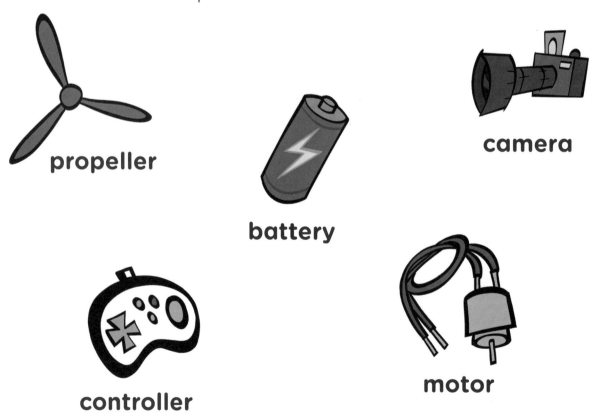

propeller

battery

camera

controller

motor

DESIGN ON NEXT PAGE

Design your own drone here.

ANSWER KEY

PAGE 38-39

A	B	C	D	E	F
G	H	I	J	K	L
M	N	O	P	Q	R
S	T	U	V	W	X
Y	Z				

PAGE 43

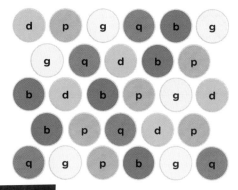

PAGE 118

Your answers might include:

cab, dab, jab, lab,
bat, cat, hat, sat,
bad, dad, mad, sad,
ban, man, pan, van,
bag, hag, nag, rag,
cap, gap, map, rap,
bam, ham, jam, yam,
gal, pal, yak, wax

PAGE 119

Your answers might include:

bed, fed, red, led,
beg, leg, peg,
bet, get, jet, pet,
den, hen men, pen

PAGE 120

Your answers might include:

bit, fit, kit, sit,
bid, did, kid, lid,
big, dig, gig, wig,
dim, him, rim,
dip, hip, lip, zip,
bin, pin, sin, tin

PAGE 121

Your answers might include:

cot, dot, hot, pot,
cob, job, mob, sob,
cog, dog, hog, jog,
cop, hop, mop, top,
box, fox, mom

PAGE 122

Your answers might include:

but, cut, gut, nut,
cub, rud, sub, tub,
bug, dug, jug, rug,
bum, gum, mum, sum,
bun, fun, nun, sun,
bud, dud, mud,
pup, cup, bus

PAGE 123

1. **kiss**

2. **bell**

3. **buzz**

4. **duck**

5. **mess**

6. **dress**

PAGE 124-125

1. **cat**
2. **jump**
3. **hand**
4. **back**
5. **wish**
6. **red**
7. **box**
8. **fish**
9. **egg**
10. **bus**

PAGE 128-129

Non-real words:

3. **hig**
4. **fim**
5. **mub**
10. **mab**
12. **mup**
18. **dat**
19. **mit**

PAGE 132-133

Non-real words:

4. **kezz**
11. **juck**
12. **zoth**
13. **coss**
14. **shup**
16. **rell**

PAGE 136

small

PAGE 137

sad

PAGE 138-139

1. **on**
2. **in**
3. **beneath**
4. **behind**
5. **in front of**
6. **next to**

PAGE 146

PAGE 147

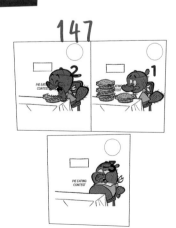

PAGE 148

PAGE 149

PAGE 150

PAGE 151

1. **happy**

2. **crying**

3. **angry**

4. **laughing**

5. **sad**

PAGE 162–163

1. **1 sheep**
2. **2 sheep**
3. **3 sheep**
4. **4 sheep**
5. **5 sheep**
6. **6 sheep**
7. **7 sheep**
8. **8 sheep**
9. **9 sheep**
10. **10 sheep**

PAGE 164–165

1. **3 cakes**
2. **7 doughnuts**
3. **4 balloons**
4. **9 candles**
5. **5 party hats**
6. **6 presents**
7. **2 pizzas**
8. **1 piñata**

PAGE 166–167

1. **3 cookies**
2. **6 cookies**
3. **4 cookies**
4. **5 cookies**
5. **8 cookies**
6. **7 cookies**
7. **2 cookies**
8. **9 cookies**

PAGE 168–169

1. **10 bees**
2. **5 cows**
3. **3 sheep**
4. **4 fish**
5. **9 ants**
6. **6 wolves**

1.
2.
3.
4.

1.
2.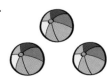
3.
4.

1.
2.
3.
4.
5.
6.

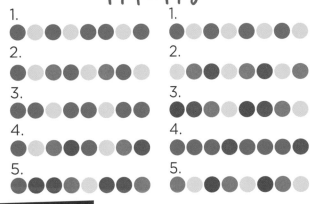

1.
2.
3.
4.
5.

1.
2.
3.
4.
5.

1. **1 + 9 = 10**
2. **2 + 8 = 10**
3. **3 + 7 = 10**
4. **4 + 6 = 10**
5. **5 + 5 = 10**

1. ■ square
2. ● circle
3. ⬡ heptagon
4. ⬡ octagon
5. ⬣ hexagon
6. ⬠ pentagon
7. ⬭ oval
8. ▲ triangle
9. ▯ rectangle
10. ◇ rhombus

MEET THE
MRS WORDSMITH TEAM

Editor-in-Chief
Sofia Fenichell

Associate Creative Director
Lady San Pedro

Art Director
Craig Kellman

Writers

Tatiana Barnes

Mark Holland
Sawyer Eaton

Amelia Mehra

Researcher
Eleni Savva

Lexicographer
Ian Brookes

Designers

Suzanne Bullat
James Sales

Fabrice Gourdel
James Webb
Holly Jones

Caroline Henriksen
Jess Macadam

Producers
Eva Schumacher Payne
Leon Welters

Academic Advisors
Emma Madden
Prof. Susan Neuman

Project Managers
Senior Editor Helen Murray
Design Manager Sunita Gahir

Senior Production Editor Jennifer Murray
Senior Production Controller Louise Minihane
Publishing Director Mark Searle

DK Delhi
DTP Designers Satish Gaur and Rohit Rojal
Senior DTP Designer Pushpak Tyagi
Pre-production Manager Sunil Sharma
Managing Art Editor Romi Chakraborty

DK would like to thank Roohi Sehgal and Julia March
for editorial assistance.

First published in Great Britain in 2021 by
Dorling Kindersley Limited
A Penguin Random House Company
DK, One Embassy Gardens, 8 Viaduct Gardens,
London, SW11 7BW

The authorised representative in the EEA is
Dorling Kindersley Verlag GmbH. Arnulfstr. 124,
80636 Munich, Germany.

Variations of this content are available as
printable worksheets at mrswordsmith.com

10 9 8 7 6 5 4 3 2
004-325946-August/2021

© 2021 Mrs Wordsmith

A CIP catalogue record for this book
is available from the British Library.
ISBN 978-0-24152-710-8

Printed and bound in Malaysia

www.dk.com

mrswordsmith.com

For the curious

The building blocks of reading

READ TO LEARN

LEARN TO READ

| Phonemic Awareness | Phonics | Fluency | Vocabulary | Reading Comprehension |

READICULOUS

Readiculous App
App Store & Google Play

WORD TAG
Los Angeles

Word Tag App
App Store & Google Play

OUR JOB IS TO INCREASE YOUR CHILD'S READING AGE

This book adheres to the science of reading. Our research-backed learning helps children progress through phonemic awareness, phonics, fluency, vocabulary, and reading comprehension.